GANKAKU, JION

BEST KARATE 8

Gankaku, Jion

M. Nakayama

KODANSHA INTERNATIONAL LTD.

Tokyo, New York & San Francisco

Front cover photo by Keizō Kaneko; demonstration photos by Yoshinao Murai.

Distributed in the United States by Kodansha International/USA, Ltd. through Harper & Row, Publishers, Inc., 10 East 53rd Street, New York, New York 10022.

Published by Kodansha International Ltd., 12–21 Otowa 2-chome, Bunkyo-ku, Tokyo 112 and Kodansha International/USA, Ltd., 10 East 53rd Street, New York, New York 10022 and 44 Montgomery Street, San Francisco, California 94104. Copyright © 1981 by Kodansha International Ltd. All rights reserved. Printed in Japan.

LCC 77-74827
ISBN 0-87011-402-6
JBC 2375-789068-2361

First edition, 1981

CONTENTS

Dedicated
to my teacher
GICHIN FUNAKOSHI

INTRODUCTION

The past decade has seen a great increase in the popularity of karate-dō throughout the world. Among those who have been attracted to it are college students and teachers, artists, businessmen and civil servants. It has come to be practiced by policemen and members of Japan's Self-defense Forces. In a number of universities, it has become a compulsory subject, and that number is increasing yearly.

Along with the increase in popularity, there have been certain unfortunate and regrettable interpretations and performances. For one thing, karate has been confused with the so-called Chinese-style boxing, and its relationship with the original Okinawan *Te* has not been sufficiently understood. There are also people who have regarded it as a mere show, in which two men attack each other savagely, or the contestants battle each other as though it were a form of boxing in which the feet are used, or a man shows off by breaking bricks or other hard objects with his head, hand or foot.

If karate is practiced solely as a fighting technique, this is cause for regret. The fundamental techniques have been developed and perfected through long years of study and practice, but to make any effective use of these techniques, the spiritual aspect of this art of self-defense must be recognized and must play the predominant role. It is gratifying to me to see that there are those who understand this, who know that karate-dō is a purely Oriental martial art, and who train with the proper attitude.

To be capable of inflicting devastating damage on an opponent with one blow of the fist or a single kick has indeed been the objective of this ancient Okinawan martial art. But even the practitioners of old placed stronger emphasis on the spiritual side of the art than on the techniques. Training means training of body and spirit, and, above all else, one should treat his opponent courteously and with the proper etiquette. It is not enough to fight with all one's power, the real objective in karate-dō is to do so for the sake of justice.

Gichin Funakoshi, a great master of karate-dō, pointed out repeatedly that the first purpose in pursuing this art is the nurturing of a sublime spirit, a spirit of humility. Simultaneously, power sufficient to destroy a ferocious wild animal with a single blow should be developed. Becoming a true follower of karate-dō is possible only when one attains perfection in these two aspects, the one spiritual, the other physical.

Karate as an art of self-defense and karate as a means of improving and maintaining health has long existed. During the past twenty years, a new activity has been explored and is coming to the fore. This is *sports karate.*

In sports karate, contests are held for the purpose of determining the ability of the participants. This needs emphasizing, for here again there is cause for regret. There is a tendency to place too much emphasis on winning contests, and those who do so neglect the practice of fundamental techniques, opting instead to attempt jiyū kumite at the earliest opportunity.

Emphasis on winning contests cannot help but alter the fundamental techniques a person uses and the practice he engages in. Not only that, it will result in a person's being incapable of executing a strong and effective technique, which, after all, is the unique characteristic of karate-dō. The man who begins jiyū kumite prematurely—without having practiced fundamentals sufficiently—will soon be overtaken by the man who has trained in the basic techniques long and diligently. It is, quite simply, a matter of haste makes waste. There is no alternative to learning and practicing basic techniques and movements step by step, stage by stage.

If karate competitions are to be held, they must be conducted under suitable conditions and in the proper spirit. The desire to win a contest is counterproductive, since it leads to a lack of seriousness in learning the fundamentals. Moreover, aiming for a savage display of strength and power in a contest is totally undesirable. When this happens, courtesy toward the opponent is forgotten, and this is of prime importance in any expression of karate. I believe this matter deserves a great deal of reflection and self-examination by both instructors and students.

To explain the many and complex movements of the body, it has been my desire to present a fully illustrated book with an up-to-date text, based on the experience in this art that I have acquired over a period of forty-six years. This hope is being realized by the publication of the *Best Karate* series, in which earlier writings of mine have been totally revised with the help and encouragement of my readers. This new series explains in detail what karate-dō is in language made as simple as possible, and I sincerely hope that it will be of help to followers of karate-dō. I hope also that karateka in many countries will be able to understand each other better through this series of books.

WHAT KARATE-DŌ IS

Deciding who is the winner and who is the loser is not the ultimate objective. Karate-dō is a martial art for the development of character through training, so that the karateka can surmount any obstacle, tangible or intangible.

Karate-dō is an empty-handed art of self-defense in which the arms and legs are systematically trained and an enemy attacking by surprise can be controlled by a demonstration of strength like that of using actual weapons.

Karate-dō is exercise through which the karateka masters all body movements, such as bending, jumping and balancing, by learning to move limbs and body backward and forward, left and right, up and down, freely and uniformly.

The techniques of karate-dō are well controlled according to the karateka's will power and are directed at the target accurately and spontaneously.

The essence of karate techniques is *kime*. The meaning of *kime* is an explosive attack to the target using the appropriate technique and maximum power in the shortest time possible. (Long ago, there was the expression *ikken hissatsu*, meaning "to kill with one blow," but to assume from this that killing is the objective is dangerous and incorrect. It should be remembered that the karateka of old were able to practice *kime* daily and in dead seriousness by using the makiwara.)

Kime may be accomplished by striking, punching or kicking, but also by blocking. A technique lacking *kime* can never be regarded as true karate, no matter how great the resemblance to karate. A contest is no exception; however, it is against the rules to make contact because of the danger involved.

Sun-dome means to arrest a technique just before contact with the target (one *sun*, about three centimeters). But not carrying a technique through to *kime* is not true karate, so the question is how to reconcile the contradiction between *kime* and *sun-dome*. The answer is this: establish the target slightly in front of the opponent's vital point. It can then be hit in a controlled way with maximum power, without making contact.

Training transforms various parts of the body into weapons to be used freely and effectively. The quality necessary to accomplish this is self-control. To become a victor, one must first overcome his own self.

KATA

The *kata* of karate-dō are logical arrangements of blocking, punching, striking and kicking techniques in certain set sequences. About fifty kata, or "formal exercises," are practiced at the present time, some having been passed down from generation to generation, others having been developed fairly recently.

Kata can be divided into two broad categories. In one group are those appropriate for physical development, the strengthening of bone and muscle. Though seemingly simple, they require composure for their performance and exhibit strength and dignity when correctly performed. In the other group are kata suitable for the development of fast reflexes and the ability to move quickly. The lightninglike movements in these kata are suggestive of the rapid flight of the swallow. All kata require and foster rhythm and coordination.

Training in kata is spiritual as well as physical. In his performance of the kata, the karateka should exhibit boldness and confidence, but also humility, gentleness and a sense of decorum, thus integrating mind and body in a singular discipline. As Gichin Funakoshi often reminded his students, "The spirit of karate-dō is lost without courtesy."

One expression of this courtesy is the bow made at the beginning and at the end of each kata. The stance is the *musubi-dachi* (informal attention stance), with the arms relaxed, the hands lightly touching the thighs and the eyes focused straight ahead.

From the bow at the start of the kata, one moves into the *kamae* of the first movement of the kata. This is a relaxed position, so tenseness, particularly in the shoulders and knees, should be eliminated and breathing should be relaxed. The center of power and concentration is the *tanden*, the center of gravity. In this position, the karateka should be prepared for any eventuality and full of fighting spirit.

Being relaxed but alert also characterizes the bow at the end of the kata and is called *zanshin*. In karate-dō, as in other martial arts, bringing the kata to a perfect finish is of the greatest importance.

Each kata begins with a blocking technique and consists of a specific number of movements to be performed in a particular order. There is some variation in the complexity of the movements and the time required to complete them, but each movement has its own meaning and function and nothing is superfluous. Performance is along the *embusen* (performance line), the shape of which is decided for each kata.

While performing a kata, the karateka should imagine himself to be surrounded by opponents and be prepared to execute defensive and offensive techniques in any direction.

Mastery of kata is a prerequisite for advancement through *kyū* and *dan* as follows:

8th *kyū*	Heian 1
7th *kyū*	Heian 2
6th *kyū*	Heian 3
5th *kyū*	Heian 4
4th *kyū*	Heian 5
3rd *kyū*	Tekki 1
2nd *kyū*	Kata other than Heian or Tekki
1st *kyū*	Other than the above
1st *dan*	Other than the above
2nd *dan* and above	Free kata

Free kata may be chosen from Bassai, Kankū, Jutte, Hangetsu, Empi, Gankaku, Jion, Tekki, Nijūshihō, Gojūshihō, Unsu, Sōchin, Meikyō, Chintei, Wankan and others.

Important Points

Since the effects of practice are cumulative, practice every day, even if only for a few minutes. When performing a kata, keep calm and never rush through the movements. This means always being aware of the correct timing of each movement. If a particular kata proves difficult, give it more attention, and always keep in mind the relationship between kata practice and kumite (see Vols. 3 and 4).

Specific points in performance are:

1. *Correct order*. The number and sequence of movements is predetermined. All must be performed.

2. *Beginning and end*. The kata must begin and end at the same spot on the *embusen*. This requires practice.

3. *Meaning of each movement*. Each movement, defensive or offensive must be clearly understood and fully expressed. This is also true of the kata as a whole, each of which has its own characteristics.

4. *Awareness of the target*. The karateka must know what the target is and when to execute a technique.

5. *Rhythm and timing*. Rhythm must be appropriate to the particular kata and the body must be flexible, never overstrained. Remember the three factors of the correct use of power, swiftness or slowness in executing techniques, and the stretching and contraction of muscles.

6. *Proper breathing*. Breathing should change with changing situations, but basically inhale when blocking, exhale

when a finishing technique is executed, and inhale and exhale when executing successive techniques.

Related to breathing is the *kiai*, which occurs in the middle or at the end of the kata, at the moment of maximum tension. By exhaling very sharply and tensing the abdomen, extra power can be given to the muscles.

Standardization

The basic kata, Heian and Tekki, and the free kata from Bassai to Jion are all the essentially important Shōto-kan kata. In 1948, disciples from Keio, Waseda and Takushoku universities met with Master Gichin Funakoshi at Waseda University. Their purpose was to form a viewpoint for the unification of the kata, which in the period after the war had been subject to varied individual and subjective interpretations. The kata as presented in *Best Karate* embody the criteria for standardization established at that time.

Rhythm

GANKAKU

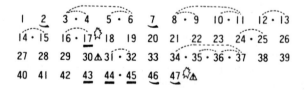

JION

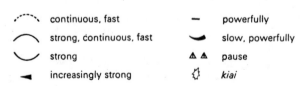

⸛	continuous, fast	— powerfully
⌢	strong, continuous, fast	⌣ slow, powerfully
⌣	strong	▲ ▲ pause
◄	increasingly strong	♧ *kiai*

GANKAKU

1

Yōi

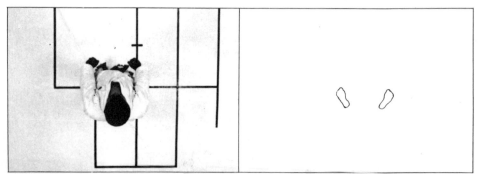

Shizen-tai

Ryō shō jōdan sokumen awase-uke

Upper level augmented side block with both hands Left leg
is pivot; rotate hips to right, bringing right foot back one step.

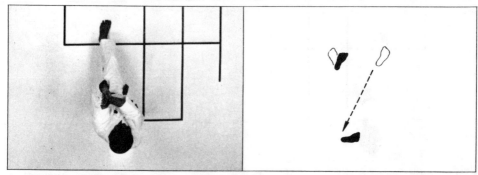

1. Migi kōkutsu-dachi

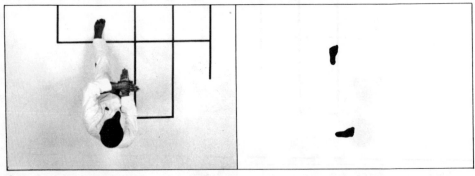

Middle level pressing block with both hands   Both hands as they are, turn wrists over in front of right side, left hand on top.

2.

18

3 Hidari ken chūdan-zuki

Middle level punch with left fist

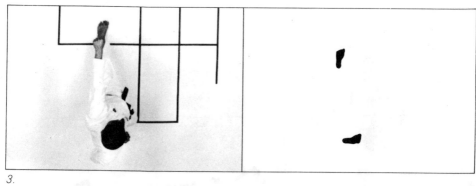

3.

4 *Migi ken chūdan gyaku-zuki*

Middle level reverse punch with right fist

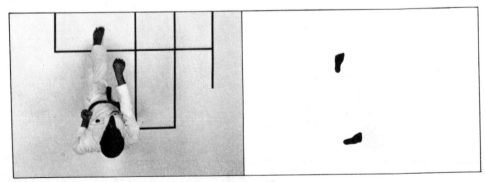

4.

5 Migi sokumen gedan-barai

Downward block to right side

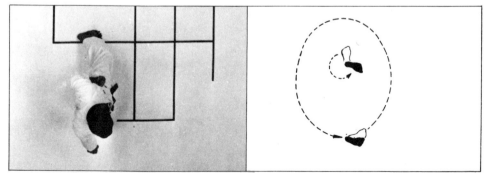

5. Kiba-dachi

6 _Ryō shō jūji jōdan kōsa-uke_

Upper level X block with both hands

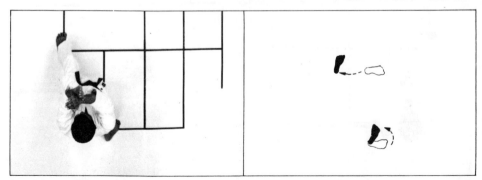

6. _Hidari zenkutsu-dachi_

7   *Ryō shō nigiri mune mae jūji kamae*

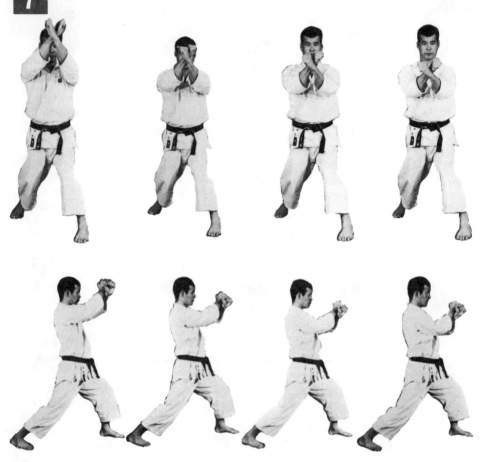

Hands clasped in front of chest X kamae   Do this slowly, with the feeling of tightening the sides of the chest.

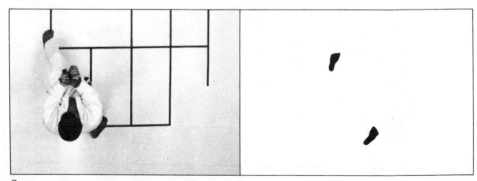

7.

8 Nidan geri

a

Two-level kick

25

8 b
Ryō ken jūji gedan kōsa-uke

Lower level X block with both fists

8b. Hidari zenkutsu-dachi

Ryō ken jūji gedan kōsa-uke

Lower level X block with both fists Keeping wrists crossed rotate hips to right with right leg as pivot.

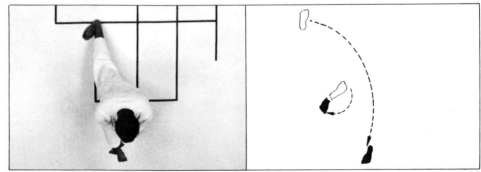

9. *Hidari zenkutsu-dachi*

10

Migi ken gedan uke
Hidari ken migi koshi mae kamae

Lower level block with right fist/Left fist at right side kamae
Left leg is pivot; rotate hips to right.

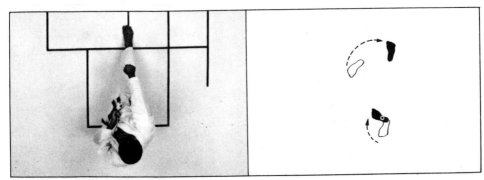

10. Hidari kōkutsu-dachi

11 Hidari shutō gedan uke
Migi shutō hidari koshi mae kamae

Lower level block with left sword hand/Right sword hand at left side kamae   Do this slowly.

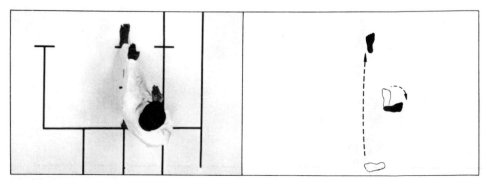

11. Migi kōkutsu-dachi

Ryō shō chūdan kakiwake uke

Middle level reverse wedge block with both hands Backs of both hands to the rear. Rotate hips to right.

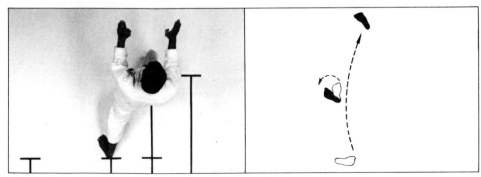

12. *Migi zenkutsu-dachi*

Middle level reverse wedge block with both hands Backs of both hands to the front.

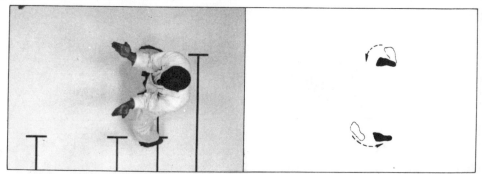

13. Kiba-dachi

14

Ryō te o kakiwake oroshi sahō o miru
Sono mama hiza o nobasu

Downward thrust with both hands/Look to left Straighten knees.

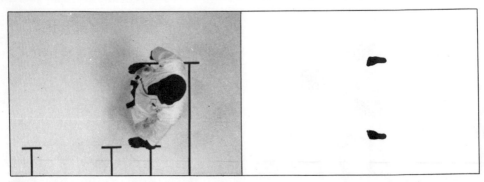

14.

15 Migi sokumen jōdan uchi uke
Hidari sokumen gedan uke

Upper level block, inside outward, to right side/Lower level block to left side Bring left hand from in front of right shoulder, right hand from under left elbow in a twisting motion.

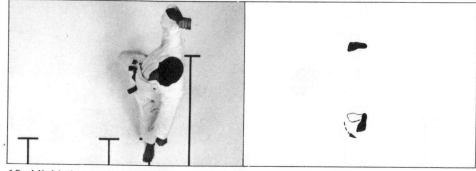

15. Migi kōkutsu-dachi

16 *Hidari sokumen jōdan uchi uke*
Migi sokumen gedan uke

*Upper level block, inside outward, to left side/Lower level block
to right side* Left leg is pivot; rotate hips to left.

16. Hidari kōkutsu-dachi

17 *Migi sokumen jōdan uchi uke*
Hidari sokumen gedan uke

Upper level block, inside outward, to right side/Lower level block to left side   Right leg is pivot; rotate hips to left.

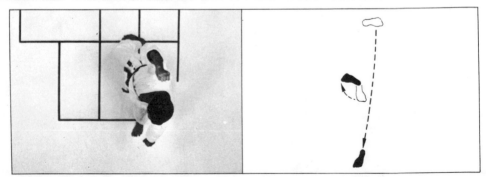

17. *Migi kōkutsu-dachi*

Ryō ken jūji gedan kōsa-uke

Lower level X block with both hands Right hand on top.
Kneel on right knee, left knee bent.

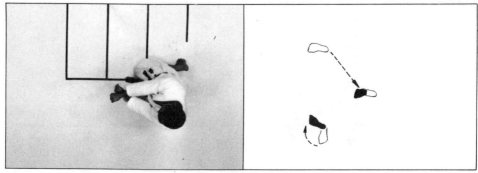

18.

Middle level reverse wedge (*block*)   Backs of fists to the front.
Do this slowly.

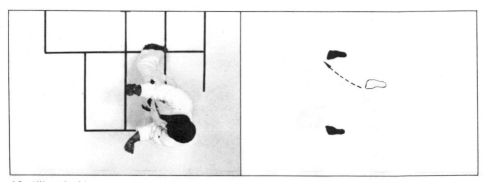

19. Kiba-dachi

Ryō ken kakiwake orosu

Downward thrust with both fists Quietly and slowly. With
feet in place, straighten knees.

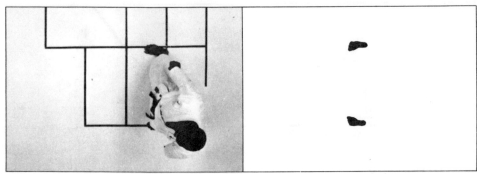

20.

Ryō ken ryō koshi

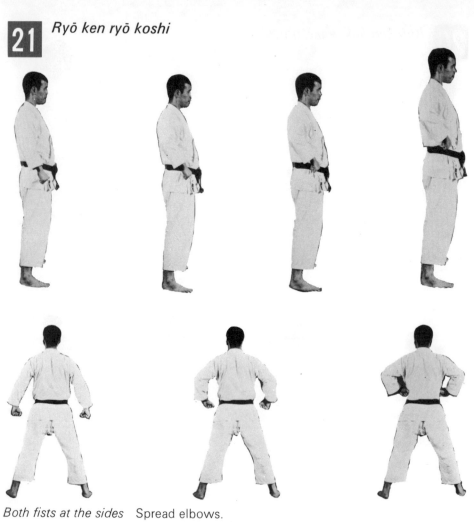

Both fists at the sides Spread elbows.

21.

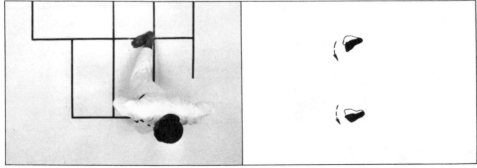

Right elbow strike Bend left knee ; straighten right knee.

22.

23 *Hidari hiji-ate*

Left elbow strike   Bend right knee; straighten left knee.

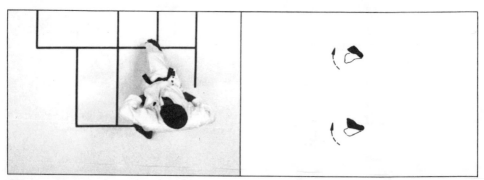

23.

24 *Ryō ken chūdan kakiwake*

Middle level reverse wedge block   Backs of fists to the front.
Cross left leg in back of right heel.

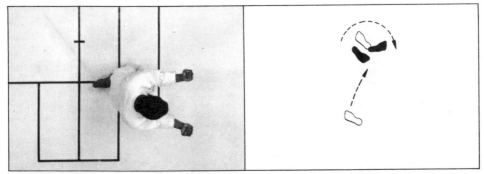

24. *Kōsa-dachi*

Migi sokumen jōdan uchi uke kamae
Hidari sokumen gedan-gamae

Upper level block-kamae, inside outward, to right side/Lower
level kamae to left side   Gradually raise hips, apply power.

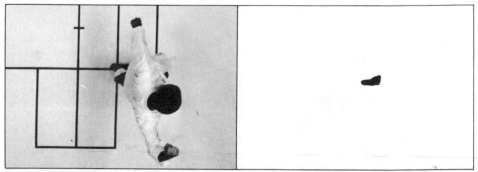

25. *Migi ashi-dachi*

26 *Ryō ken migi koshi kamae*

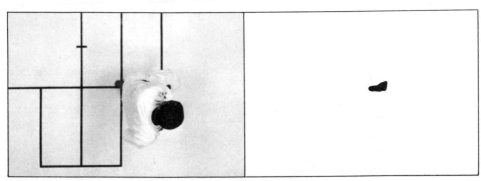

Both fists at right side kamae   Instantly withdraw power.

26.

27 Hidari uraken jōdan yoko mawashi-uchi
Hidari sokutō chūdan yoko keage

Upper level horizontal strike with left back-fist/Middle level side snap kick with left sword foot

27.

28 *Migi ken chūdan oi-zuki*

EI!!

Middle level lunge punch with right fist

28. Migi zenkutsu-dachi

Hidari sokumen jōdan uke kamae
Migi sokumen gedan-gamae

Upper level block-kamae to left side/Lower level kamae to right side Right foot to back of left knee. Gradually raise hips, apply power.

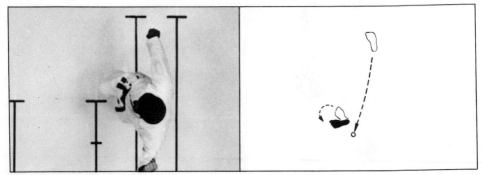

29. Hidari ashi-dachi

Ryō ken hidari koshi kamae

Both fists left side kamae   Instantly withdraw power.

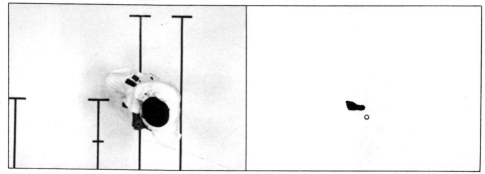

30.

31

Migi uraken jōdan yoko mawashi-uchi
Migi sokutō chūdan yoko keage

Upper level horizontal strike with right back-fist/Middle level
side snap kick with right sword foot

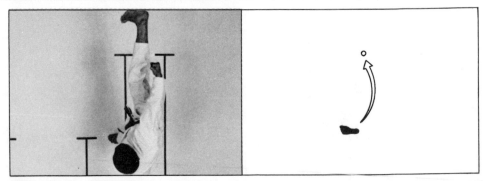

31.

32 Hidari ken migi sokumen chūdan-zuki
Migi ken migi koshi

Middle level punch to right side with left fist / Right fist at right side

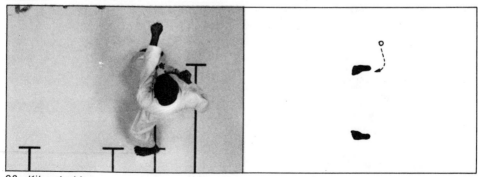

32. Kiba-dachi

33

Migi sokumen jōdan uchi uke kamae
Hidari sokumen gedan-gamae

Upper level block-kamae, inside outward, to right side/Lower level kamae to left side   Left foot to back of right knee.

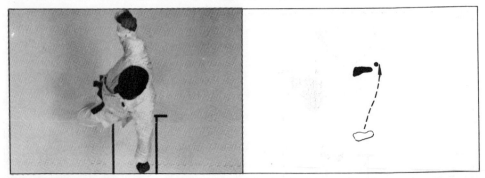

33. Migi ashi-dachi

Both fists right side kamae

34.

Upper level horizontal strike with left back-fist/Middle level
side snap kick with left sword foot

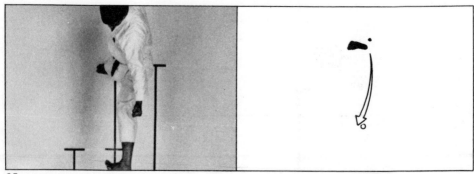

35.

36 *Migi ken hidari sokumen chūdan-zuki*

Middle level punch to left side with right fist

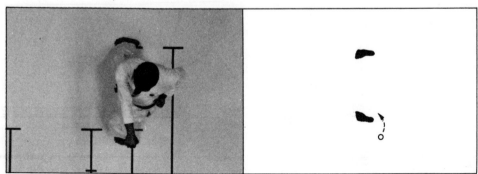

36. *Kiba-dachi*

Migi shutō migi sokumen jōdan yoko uke

Upper level side block to right side with right sword hand   Do while turning head to right.

37.

Hidari tate empi jōdan uchi

Upper level left upward elbow strike Rotate hips to right with feeling of rooted stance. Strike right fist with left elbow.

38.

39

Hidari shō hidari koshi
Migi ken hidari shō ni oshi-ateru

Left hand to left side/Push right fist against left hand Right palm inward. Rapidly rotate hips to left.

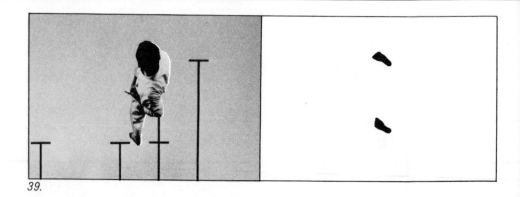

39.

Ryō ken migi koshi kamae
Hidari ken o migi ken ni kasaneru

Both fists to right side kamae/Left fist on right fist While bringing palm-heels together and turning wrists over, swing hands high above head.

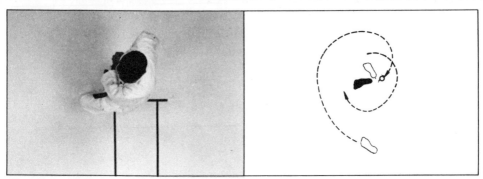

40. Migi ashi-dachi

41

Hidari uraken jōdan yoko mawashi-uchi
Hidari sokutō chūdan yoko keage

Upper level horizontal strike with left back-fist/Middle level side snap kick with left sword foot

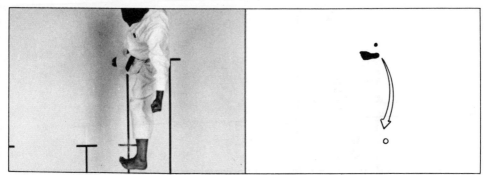

41.

42 *Migi ken chūdan oi-zuki*

Middle level lunge punch with right fist

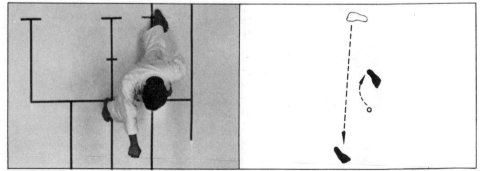

42. *Migi zenkutsu-dachi*

Naore

With right leg as pivot, turn left, withdraw left leg to return to posture of *yōi*.

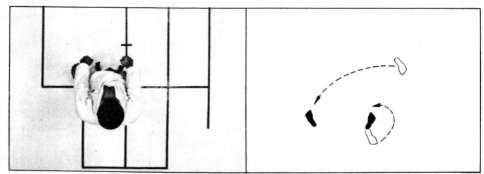

Shizen-tai

GANKAKU : IMPORTANT POINTS ▬▬▬▬

This is the kata formerly called Chintō. It takes its present name, "Crane on a Rock," from the postures that are just like a crane standing on one leg on a rock, ready to pounce on an enemy. When in this posture, one should have the feeling of inhibiting and overpowering the enemy's movements.

With the *yoko keage* as its special nucleus, this is an unparalleled kata. It is appropriate for mastering balance while standing on one leg and simultaneously counterattacking with the side kick and back-fist.

Forty-two movements. About one minute.

1. Movements 1–2: This is used primarily against an attack to the head coming from the side. Simultaneously withdraw right leg, rotate hips rapidly to right, and apply the augmented block with the backs of both fists coming vertical. Rotation of hips and the direction of the block are opposite.

In using the right hand to the left side, push the left hand—back to back with the right hand—strongly.

After the upper level side block against continuous body attacks, turn wrists over and knock aside punches.

3

4

2. Movements 3–4: Against a middle level strike, get inside the opponent's arm and while using the elbow for a sliding block (*suri-uke*), counterattack to the sides of his body.

3. Movement 5: With left leg as pivot, turn to left. At the same time, swing right fist from high above the head and block to the lower level. Use right leg for a strong stamping kick against the opponent's shin or the back of his leg. Raise knee high.

4. Movement 6: In the augmented forearm block, execute the rising block by describing an arc with the arms, with the feeling of a straight rising punch.

5

6

7

5. Movement 8: Trapping the attacking hand between the blocking hands is orthodox. However, blocking with the left wrist and striking the opponent's shin with the augmented right fist is also effective.

6. Movements 12–13: In the reverse wedge block, narrow the shoulders, cross wrists and slowly spread arms to the sides.

7. Movements 22–23: Block by spreading elbows and rapidly rotating hips. It is necessary to have the feeling of blocking with the hip rotation.

8

9

8. Movement 27: While striking with the back-fist, use left leg for a side snap kick—back-fist to the temple, sword foot to the side of the body. Thrust kick is most effective for longer distances, snap kick for shorter distances.

9. Movements 37–38: After upper level sword hand block, grab opponent's wrist and pull upward to break his balance and attack to the jaw with an upward elbow strike. It is important to slide the foot forward before turning the hip on the side of the striking elbow.

10. Movements 39–40: Blocking a face attack, grasp the opponent's wrist and pull toward the left hip. While turning to right on right leg, bring both hands from high above the head with the feeling of shouldering something and get inside the opponent's arm. Coordinate turning the body with swinging the arms.

$$\frac{2}{\text{JION}}$$

Yōi

Wrap left hand around right fist, bring hands in front of jaw for *kamae*. Backs of hands outward.

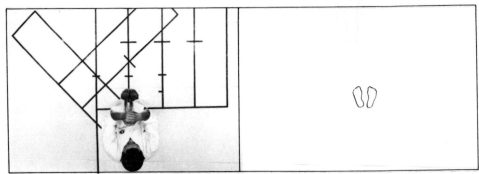

Heisoku-dachi

1

Migi ken chūdan uchi uke
Hidari ken gedan uke

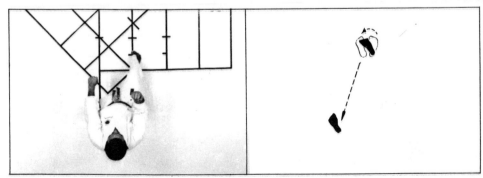

Middle level block, inside outward, with right fist/Lower level block with left fist Quickly bring right fist from under left elbow, left fist from right shoulder.

1. *Migi zenkutsu-dachi*

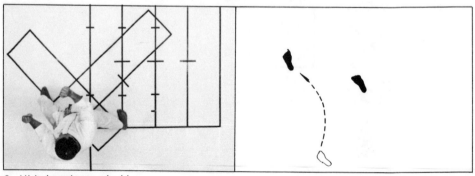

Middle level reverse wedge (*block*) Backs of hands diagonally outward. Move left leg and hands slowly, at the same time. Twisting both wrists, cross them in front of chest.

2. *Hidari zenkutsu-dachi*

Migi chūdan mae keage

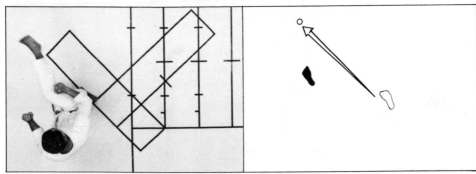

Right middle level front kick When kicking, do not change position of elbows from that of reverse wedge block.

3.

4 Migi chūdan oi-zuki
Hidari ken hidari koshi

Right middle level lunge punch/Left fist at left side   Stamp kick to front with right foot. Do Movements 3 and 4 in one breath.

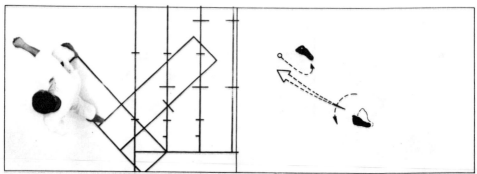

4. Migi zenkutsu-dachi

Left middle level reverse punch

Right middle level lunge punch
Do Movements 5 and 6 in one breath.

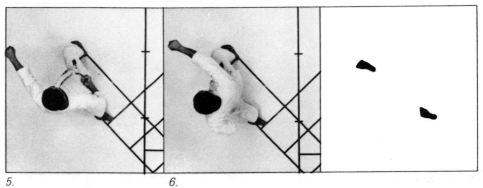

5.

6.

7 Ryō ken chūdan kakiwake

Middle level reverse wedge (*block*)   Pivot on left leg. Move
hands and feet slowly.

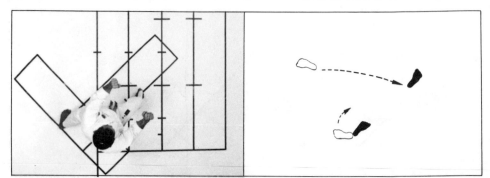

7. *Migi zenkutsu-dachi*

8 Hidari chūdan mae keage

Left middle level front kick

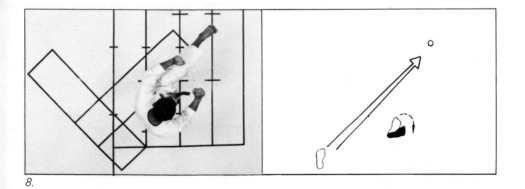

8.

Hidari chūdan oi-zuki

Left middle level lunge punch Do Movements 8 and 9 in one breath.

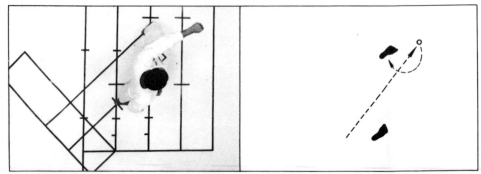

9. Hidari zenkutsu-dachi

10 *Migi chūdan gyaku-zuki*

11 *Hidari chūdan oi-zuki*

Right middle level reverse punch

Left middle level lunge punch
Do Movements 10 and 11 in one breath.

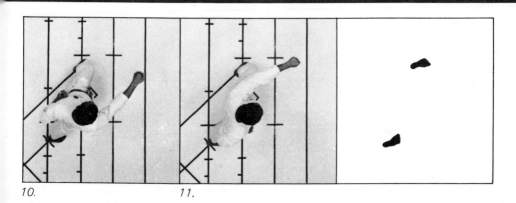

10.

11.

12 Hidari jōdan age-uke

Left upper level rising block Raise right hand in front of head, then bring it to right hip.

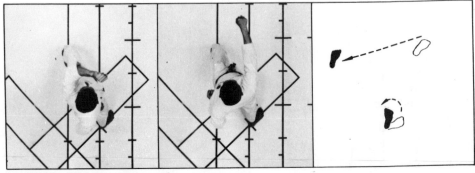

12. *Hidari zenkutsu-dachi*   13.

13 *Migi chūdan gyaku-zuki*

14 *Migi jōdan age-uke*

Right middle level reverse punch

Right upper level rising block

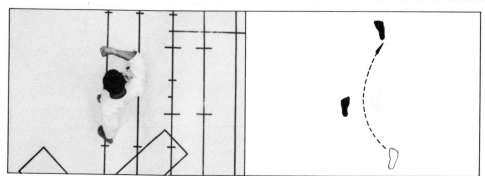

14. *Migi zenkutsu-dachi*

Left middle level reverse punch

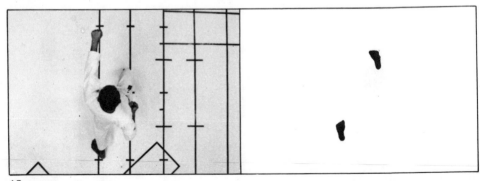

15.

16 *Hidari jōdan age-uke*

Left upper level rising block

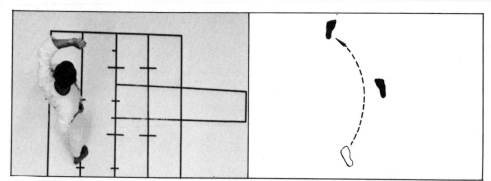

16. Hidari zenkutsu-dachi

17 *Migi chūdan oi-zuki*

Right middle level lunge punch

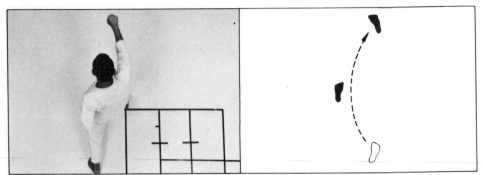

17. *Migi zenkutsu-dachi*

18 *Migi ken migi sokumen jōdan uchi uke*
Hidari ken hidari sokumen gedan uke

Upper level block, inside outward, to right side with right fist/
Lower level block to left side with left fist   Right leg is pivot;

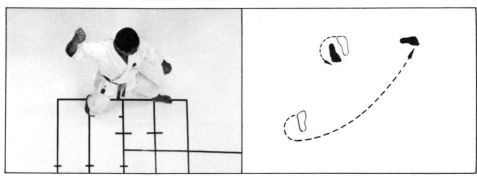

18. *Migi kōkutsu-dachi*

rotate hips to right. Bring left hand from right shoulder and
right hand from under left elbow in a twisting motion.

Migi ken kagi-zuki
Hidari ken hidari koshi

Hook punch with right fist/Left fist at left side Fist level in
front of chest, back upward. *Yori-ashi* to take stance.

19. Kiba-dachi

20 Hidari ken hidari sokumen jōdan uchi uke
Migi ken migi sokumen gedan uke

Upper level block, inside outward, to left side with left fist/
Lower level block to right side with right fist Turn head to
right.

20. Hidari kōkutsu-dachi

21 *Hidari ken kagi-zuki*
Migi ken migi koshi

Hook punch with left fist/Right fist at right side Left fist level
in front of chest, back upward. *Yori-ashi* to take straddle-leg
stance.

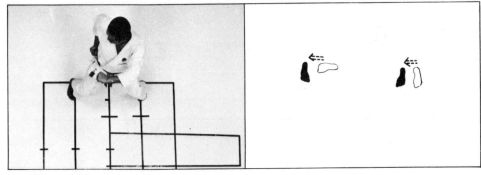

21. *Kiba-dachi*

22 *Hidari ken gedan barai*

Downward block with left fist

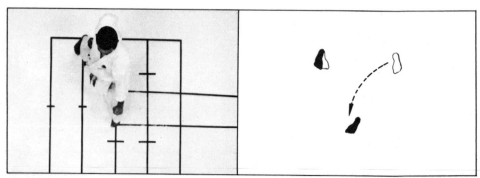

22. *Hidari zenkutsu-dachi*

Migi teishō migi sokumen chūdan yoko uke

Middle level block to right side with right palm-heel Back of
right hand outward, wrist fully bent.

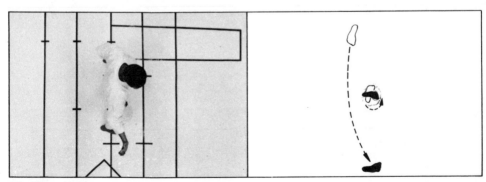

23. *Kiba-dachi*

Middle level block to left side with left palm-heel Right leg is pivot; rotate hips to right.

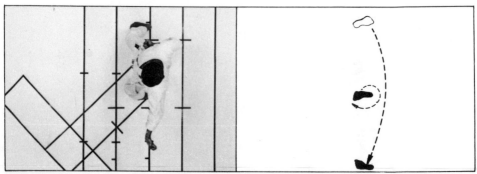

24. *Kiba-dachi*

Migi teishō migi sokumen chūdan yoko uke

Middle level block to right side with right palm-heel Rotate
hips to left.

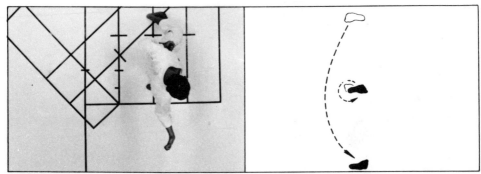

25. Kiba-dachi

26 *Migi ken migi sokumen jōdan uchi uke*
Hidari ken hidari sokumen gedan uke

Upper level block, inside outward, to right side with right fist/
Lower level block to left side with left fist Turn head to left.

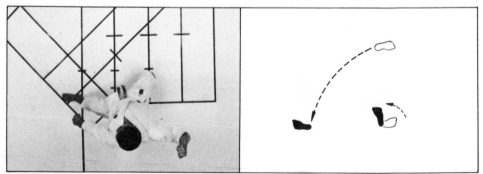

26. *Migi kōkutsu-dachi*

Hidari ken hidari sokumen morote jōdan uchi uke
Migi ken hidari hiji mae-zoe

Upper level augmented block, inside outward, to left side with
left fist/Right fist at front of left elbow

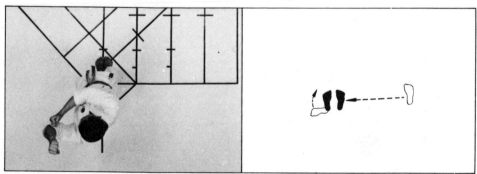

27. Heisoku-dachi

28 Hidari ken hidari sokumen jōdan uchi uke
Migi ken migi sokumen gedan uke

Upper level block, inside outward, to left side with left fist/ Lower level block to right side with right fist Turn head to right. Cross hands.

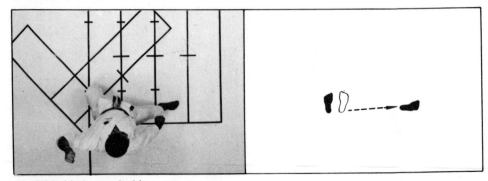

28. Hidari kōkutsu-dachi

29 Migi ken migi sokumen morote jōdan uchi uke
Hidari ken migi hiji mae-zoe

Upper level augmented block, inside outward, to right side with right fist/Left fist at front of right elbow

29. Heisoku-dachi

30 *Ryō ken ryō soku ni kakiwake orosu*

Thrust both fists down to the sides While turning head quietly to the front, thrust hands down slowly, backs of fists outward.

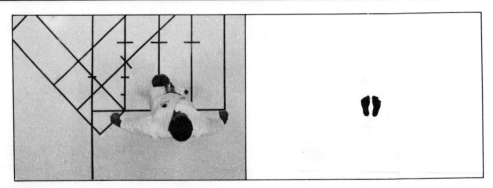

30.

31 Ryō ken gedan jūji uke

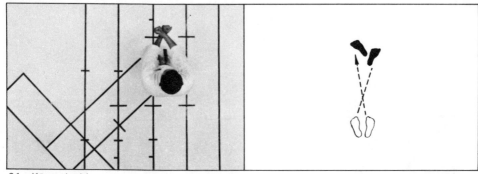

Lower level X block Jump forward from right foot. Right hand on top for X block. Backs of fists inward.

31. *Kōsa-dachi*

Ryō ken ryō soku gedan kakiwake

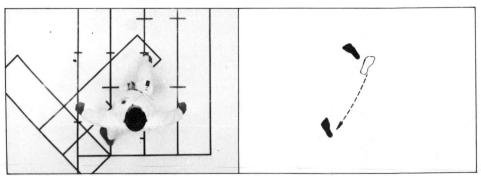

Lower level reverse wedge (block) to both sides Backs of fists outward. Take one step backward with left foot.

32. *Migi zenkutsu-dachi*

Ryō ken chūdan kakiwake-uke

Middle level reverse wedge block with both fists Starting with wrists in front of chest, execute with right fist on top.

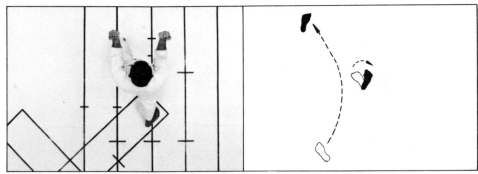

33. *Hidari zenkutsu-dachi*

Ryō ken jōdan jūji uke

Upper level X block   Right wrist in front.

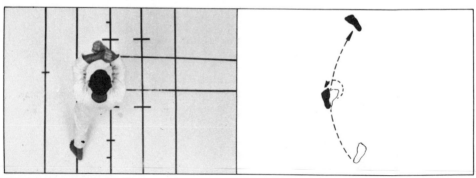

34. Migi zenkutsu-dachi

35 *Migi uraken jōdan uchi*
Hidari ken sono mama

Upper level strike with right back-fist/Left fist as is

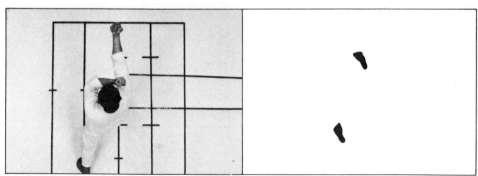

35.

36

Hidari ken chūdan tsuki-uke
Migi ken migi kata ue kamae

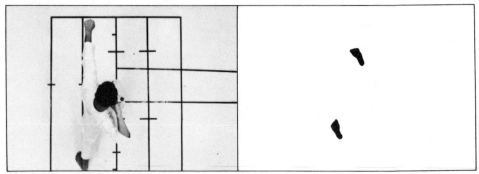

Middle level punch-block with left fist/Right fist above right shoulder kamae Back of left fist upward. Back of right fist outward.

36.

37 Migi uraken jōdan ura-zuki
Hidari ude suigetsu mae kamae

Upper level close punch with right back-fist/Left arm in front of chest kamae Back of right fist upward. Right elbow touching left wrist.

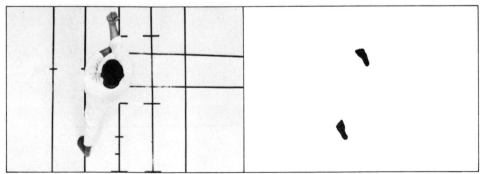

37.

38 Hidari ken chūdan uchi uke
Migi ken migi koshi

Middle level block, inside outward, with left fist/Right fist at right side   Right leg is pivot; rotate hips to left.

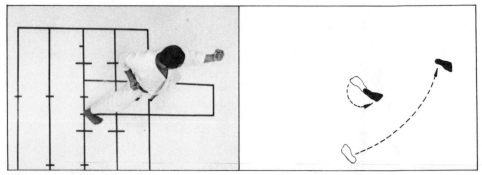

38. *Hidari zenkutsu-dachi*

39 *Migi chūdan oi-zuki*

Right middle level lunge punch

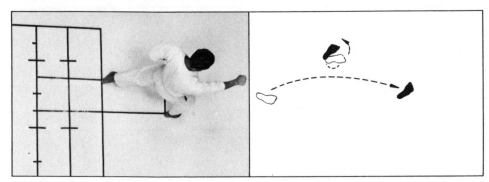

39. Migi zenkutsu-dachi

40 *Migi ken chūdan uchi uke*

Middle level block, inside outward, with right fist   Left leg is pivot ; rotate hips to right.

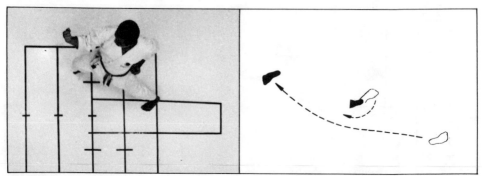

40. Migi zenkutsu-dachi

Hidari chūdan oi-zuki

Left middle level lunge punch

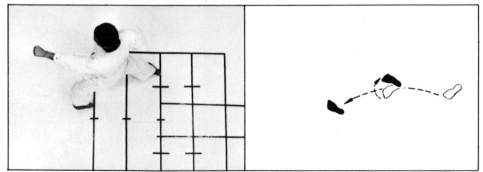

41. Hidari zenkutsu-dachi

Left downward block   Right leg is pivot; rotate hips to left.

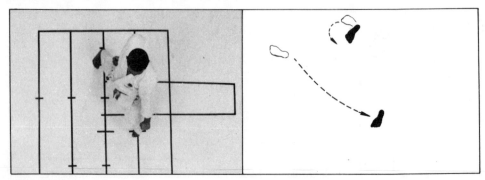

42. *Hidari zenkutsu-dachi*

Migi ken migi sokumen chūdan uchi-otoshi
Hidari ken hidari koshi

Middle level falling strike to right side with right fist/Left fist at left side Left leg is pivot; rotate hips to left. Strong stamping kick with right leg. Raise right fist and knee at the same time.

43. Kiba-dachi

Hidari ken hidari sokumen chūdan uchi-otoshi

Middle level falling strike to left side with left fist Stamping kick with left foot.

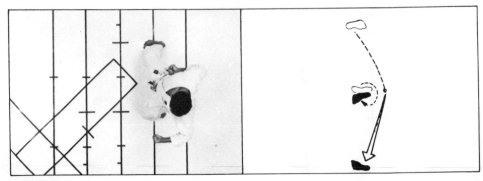

44. Kiba-dachi

45 *Migi ken migi sokumen chūdan uchi-otoshi*

Middle level falling strike to right side with right fist   Stamping
kick with right foot.

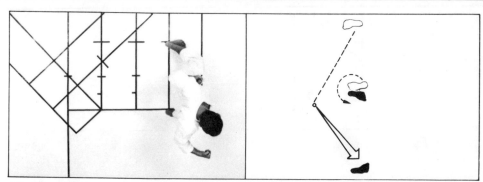

45. *Kiba-dachi*

46 Migi ken migi chichi mae
Hidari ken hidari sokumen chūdan-zuki

Right fist in front of right nipple/Middle level strike to left side with left fist Turn head to left.

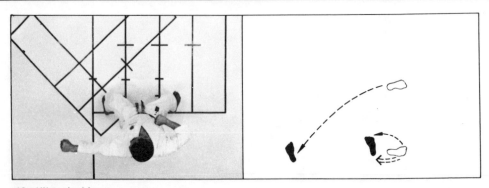

46. *Kiba-dachi*

116

47 Hidari ken hidari chichi mae
Migi ken migi sokumen chūdan-zuki

Left fist in front of left nipple/Middle level strike to right side with right fist Yori-ashi to right. Turn head to right.

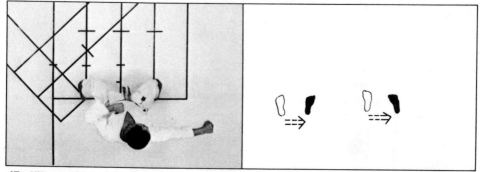

47. Kiba-dachi

Naore

Withdraw right leg to return to posture of *yōi*.

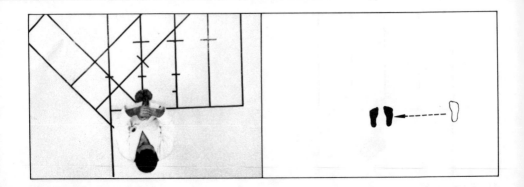

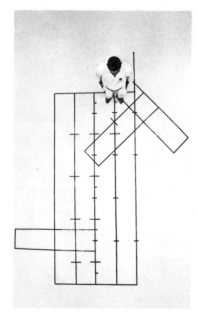

The name Jion is found in many ancient Chinese documents, and it is possible that some form of Chinese boxing was handed down by persons associated with a temple named Jion.

There is in this kata a perfect harmony like the Buddha's and in its calm movements, a strong spirit.

It is appropriate for mastering rotational movements and shifting directions. There are no particularly difficult movements. Correctly using various stances and techniques found in Heian and Tekki, it is most valuable for mastering fast and slow tempos and the fundamentals of simultaneous arm and leg movements executed while changing directions.

Forty-seven movements. About one minute.

1   2

1. Movement 1: Do not change the position of elbows for the upper level and downward blocks. The correct position is a fist-width in front of the body. This is an application of a point mastered in Heian 3.

2. Movements 2–4: For Movement 2 tighten the sides of the body and turn the forearms over. After the reverse wedge block, execute a front kick by raising the left knee high enough to touch the left nipple. When the kicking leg comes back, press hips forward, and when it touches the floor, finish off with a strike. Do not let the upper body lean forward.

3. Movements 18–19 : Bring right upper level block and left downward block to *kime* simultaneously.

4. Movements 23–24 : Bend wrist fully, thrust palm-heel out suddenly. Put power in the wrist but do not bend fingers. To tighten the sides of the body, bend elbow. Do not let elbow go away from the body. Against either strike or stick attack, hitting the target as accurately as possible is the most effective way.

5. Movements 23–25 : These are not simply blocking techniques. Using the right (blocking) palm-heel to grasp the stick, advance left foot one step while pulling the stick in. Penetrate deeply with left palm-heel and grasp the stick. Turn the arms over to break the opponent's balance. It is very important to apply the full power of the hips.

6. Movement 25: Instead of capturing the stick, at times it is effective to counterattack with a strong strike to the opponent's elbow.

7. Movements 32–33: After the lower level X block, capture the kicking leg with right hand and, as in a reverse wedge block, pull the opponent strongly, diagonally to the rear. Do not change the position of the hips from the time of the block.

8. Movement 34: The important point in the upper level X block is to execute it with the feeling of both hands doing an upward rising strike. Tighten the sides of the body.

9

10

11

9. Movement 35 : Immediately after X block to the front, punch to the upper level with right back-fist, or finish with a close punch just below the opponent's.nose.

10. Movements 36–37 : When the opponent is moving in to attack the middle level with his right fist, block in front of the head with the left arm, then punch-block to the middle level. Against a left-hand strike to the face, block to the upper level with the arm used for the back-fist strike passing the upper side of the forearm close to the right ear. Execute a close punch to the upper level for the finishing blow, thrusting the right fist out at the same time. In the upper level sweeping block with the upper side of the forearm, the fist must be facing outward.

11. Movement 43 : Swing fist widely from above head for the middle level falling strike, with the feeling of knocking the opponent's strong middle level striking forearm downward.

12. Movements 46–47: While turning the head, capture the opponent's striking arm, opening the fist and passing it by the right shoulder. Counterattack to the side of the opponent's body at the same time with the left fist. Or at close quarters finish with a hammer fist strike to his solar plexus.

With the palm facing outward, make the grasping block with the right hand passing close above the left shoulder. Pulling back the right hand and extending the left fist must be done at the same time.

3
KATA
PERFORMANCE

SECRETS OF IMPROVING KATA PERFORMANCE

In kata training, beyond steady, persistent ordinary practice, the important point is this : not only to master the great number of techniques individually practiced in the kata, but always to understand the relationship between the techniques.

Here, the especially important points in basic techniques have been selected and are explained *photographically*.

Finish arm and leg movements simultaneously

Coordinating arm and leg movements with breathing is important.

Feet moved too fast or a slow technique will result in defeat.

If the elbow is too far from the body, power cannot be concentrated.

Whatever the block, do not change the position of the elbow
When blocking, tighten the sides of the body to the maximum, keep the elbow in place. Do not lean to left or right.

Correct elbow position.

128

If the position of the elbow is not correct, the block cannot be executed.

Open the fist after blocking
Grasp the opponent's wrist and pull to destroy his balance.

Opening the hand is for the purpose of finishing off by grasping the opponent's wrist after blocking and destroying his balance by pulling his arm.

Wrong.

Block wrist with wrist

If this is not fully mastered, many of the special points of blocking are impossible to carry out.

After making wrist contact, "wrap" the blocking wrist over the attacking wrist and push downward.

Keep the palm-heel when turning the wrist over

After the X block (as in Heian 5) and side block with both hands (as in Gankaku), turn the wrist over, but only the wrist. If power is dispersed, it is impossible to overcome the opponent.

Change direction while executing technique

For a strong stamping kick, do not change the height of the hips. Raise the knee high.

Raise knee high for stamping kick

The important point is to raise the knee high and bring the foot down strongly while rotating the hips. In this respect, it should be noted that if Heian 3 is not learned completely, the blocks, such as those against stick attacks, in Jitte cannot be mastered.

Test reliability of blocks by practicing against a stick

This means mastering the basic techniques in Jitte and putting into practice: strong and stable stances, hip rotation, tightening the sides of the body, flexibility of the elbow and so on.

136

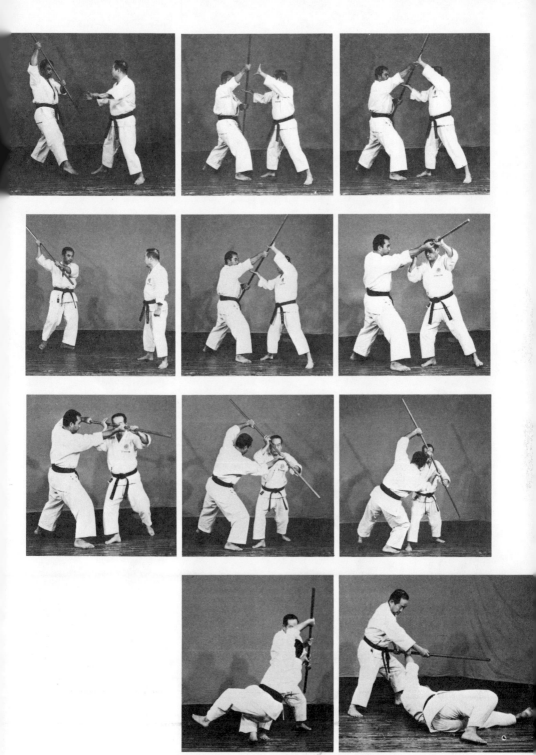

If the sides of the body are not tight, power cannot be applied.

Make the crossed-feet stance reliable

Support all the body weight on one leg.

This means making these stances in Heian 4, Kankū, Bassai and other kata strong. A plumb line from the buttocks should not go in back of the heel of the supporting leg. If the back is bent, the stance will not be effective.

Know the correct course in blocking

Thrust kick : make the knee perfectly straight.

For the side snap kick, make a short, circular jump.

Practice side snap kick and thrust kick by the right method

Strike correctly

When striking and when withdrawing the fist, the elbow should follow the same course. Tense muscles at the instant of striking, relax muscles after striking. Striking is not like thrusting out a stick. It is very important to use the snap of the elbow.

GLOSSARY

Roman numerals refer to other volumes in this series : I, Comprehensive ; II, Fundamentals ; III, Kumite 1 ; IV, Kumite 2 ; V, Heian, Tekki ; VI, Bassai, Kankū ; VII, Jitte, Hangetsu, Empi.

age-uke: rising block, 67 ; I, 70 ; II, 90, 118 ; V, 20, 28, 44

chichi: nipple, breast
chūdan: middle level
chūdan choku-zuki: middle level straight punch, 49, 76 ; I, 66 ; II, 102 ; IV, 62 ; V, 28, 126 ; VI, 27, 75 ; VII, 52, 115
chūdan mae keage: middle level front snap kick, 75, 120
chūdan osae-uke: middle level pressing block, 123 ; I, 62, 64 ; V, 37, 53, 82, 90 ; VI, 84 ; VII, 17, 19
chūdan uchi: middle level strike, 53 ; V, 94
chūdan uchi uke: middle level block, inside outward, 73, 123 ; I, 59 ; II, 22 ; V, 40 ; VI, 17, 74 ; VII, 51
chūdan yoko uke: middle level side block, 93
chūdan-zuki: middle level punch, 19, 67, 116, 123 ; V, 32 ; VI, 41, 84 ; VII, 77, 83, 86, 119, 120

dan: 13

embusen: performance line, 13 ; I, 94 ; V, 106 ; VI, 64, 138

fudō-dachi: rooted stance, 59 ; I, 35
fumikomi: stamping kick, 67, 76, 113, 136 ; I, 87 ; II, 60, 68 ; III, 33 ; V, 60 ; VI, 128

gedan barai: downward block, 21, 92 ; I, 56 ; II, 106 ; V, 17 ; VI, 48, 112 ; VII, 60, 97
gedan-gamae: lower level *kamae*, 46 ; IV, 21 ; VII, 132
gedan jūji uke: downward X block, 101. 122

gedan kōsa-uke: lower level cross block, 26
gedan uke: downward block, 29, 73, 120, 121 ; V, 50 ; VI, 43, 65, 87, 138, 140 ; VII, 37, 38
gyaku-zuki: reverse punch, 20, 77 ; I, 68 ; II, 124 ; IV, 108 ; V, 40, 48, 70, 79, 90

haiwan nagashi-uke: sweeping back-arm block, 123 ; I, 62
heisoku-dachi: informal attention stance, 72, 97 ; I, 29 ; V, 60 ; VI, 16 ; VII 16
hidari: left
hidari ashi-dachi: left leg stance, 50 ; V, 35 ; VI, 36, 79, VII, 35, 74, 112
hidari kōkutsu-dachi: left back stance, 29, 90 ; I, 31 ; II, 52 ; III, 40 ; V, 26 ; VI, 31, 72 ; VII, 38, 79, 118
hidari zenkutsu-dachi: left front stance, 23, 74 ; I, 30 ; II, 18, 52, 141 ; V, 16, 40, 58, 65, 81 ; VI, 18, 96 ; VI, 18, 101
hiji: elbow
hiji suri-uke: sliding elbow block, 67 ; II, 120
hiji-uchi: elbow strike, 43 ; I, 77 ; III, 84, 104 ; IV, 124, 126
hōkō tenkan: changing directions, 120, 135 ; II, 72 ; III, 100 ; IV, 102
hiza: knee

ikken hisatsu: to kill with one blow, 11

jinchū: point just below the nose, 123 ; I, 138
jōdan: upper level
jōdan age-uke: upper level rising

block, 82 ; I, 57 ; II, 106 ; VII, 39,
78
jōdan jūji uke: upper level X block,
104, 122, 123 ; I, 64 ; V, 64, 74, 80,
90 ; VII, 24
jōdan kōsa-uke: upper level cross
block, 23 ; VI, 131, 141
jōdan shutō uke: upper level sword
hand block, 69
jōdan uchi: upper level strike, 105
jōdan uchi uke: upper level block,
inside outward, 35, 87, 120, 121 ;
VI, 43, 87 ; VII, 37, 38
jōdan ura-zuki: upper level close
punch, 107
jōdan yoko uke: upper level side
block, 58
jūji kamae: X kamae, 24
jūji uke : X block, 134 ; I, 64 ; V, 64,
74, 80, 90

kagi-zuki: hook punch, 89 ; I, 71 ;
II, 90 ; V, 97, 106, 115, 136
kakiwake oroshi: downward thrust,
34, 100 ; VII, 30
kakiwake uke: reverse wedge block,
31, 68, 74, 102, 120, 122 ; I, 64 ;
V, 68, 74, 76
kamae: posture, 12, 47, 72 ; III, 14,
IV, 40 ; V, 32 ; VI, 12, 25, 65, 72 ;
VII, 16, 31, 59, 97, 98
kasumi: temple, 69 ; I, 138
kata: shoulder
kekomi: thrust kick, 69, 140 ; I, 86 ;
II, 82, 135 ; III, 50 ; VI, 36
ken: fist
kentsui uchi: hammer fist strike,
124 ; I, 74, 75
kiai: 14
kiba-dachi: straddle-leg stance, 21,
89 ; I, 32 ; II, 52 ; V, 54 ; VI, 44,
122 ; VII, 20, 100
kime: 11, 67, 121, 124, 126 ; I 50 ;
III, 15, IV, 118 ; V, 61 ; VII, 60
kōsa-dachi: crossed-feet stance,
101, 138 ; II, 52 ; V, 68 ; VI, 138
koshi: hip
koshi no kaiten: hip rotation, 136 ;
II, 16 ; V, 61, 75
kumite: 10, 13 ; I, 111
kuzushi: crushing (the enemy),
130 ; III, 53 ; IV, 19, 26
kyū: 13

maai: distancing, 140 ; II, 95 ; III,
14, 16, 26, 40, 72 ; IV, 18, 22, 55,
70, 112
mae: in front of
migi: right
migi ashi-dachi: right leg stance,

46 ; V, 66 ; VI, 17, 94 ; VII, 33, 75,
103
migi kokutsu-dachi: right back
stance, 17, 87 ; I, 31 ; II, 52 ; III,
40 ; V, 26 ; VI, 31, 72 ; VII, 37, 73,
119
migi zenkutsu-dachi: right front
stance, 31, 73 ; I, 30 ; II, 18, 52 ;
V, 17 ; VI, 18, 89 ; VII, 17, 128
miru: look
morote jōdan uchi uke: upper level
block, inside outward, with both
hands, 67, 97
mune: chest
musubi-dachi: informal attention
stance, 12 ; I, 29

naore: return to *yōi*
nidan geri: two-level kick, 25 ; I, 90 ;
VI, 134
nigiru: clasp

osae-uke: pressing block, 18 ; V,
129 ; VI, 84
oshi-ateru: strike

ryō: both
ryō koshi: both sides
ryō shō sokumen uke: side block
with both hands, 134
ryō soku: both sides

sahō: left direction (side)
shizen-tai: natural position, 16 ; I,
28 ; V, 16 ; VI, 16, 68, 131 ; VII,
43, 88, 96
shō: hand, palm
shutō: sword hand
sokumen: side
sokumen awase-uke: side combined
block, 17, 66 ; I, 64
sokutō: sword foot
suigetsu: solar plexus
sun-dome: arresting a technique, 11

tachikata: stance, 136 ; I, 28 ; II,
36 ; IV, 16
tanden: center of gravity, 12
tate empi uchi: upward elbow strike,
59, 69 ; I, 80 ; V, 131 ; III, 84
teishō: palm-heel
tsukami-uke: grasping block, 124 ;
V, 115 ; VI, 35, 64 ; VII, 62
tsuki-age: rising punch, 67, 122
tsuki-uke: middle level punch-block,
106, 123

uchi-otoshi: falling strike, 113, 123
ude: arm
uke kamae: block *kamae*, 46

143